I AM...

Stefka Harp

I am ...
© Stefka Mladenova 2015

All rights reserved. No part of this publication may be reproduced, stored in a retrieval system, or transmitted in any form or by any means, electronic, mechanical, photocopying, recording or otherwise, without the prior written permission of the author.

National Library of Australia Cataloguing-in-Publication entry
Creator: Harp, Stefka, author.
Title: I am .../Stafka Harp
ISBN: 978-0-9923040-7-2 (paperback)
Subjects: Emotions — Poetry
        Fear — Poetry
        Emotional Freedom Techniques
        Australian 21st century — Poetry
Dewey number: A821.4

Published with the assistance of www.wordwrightediting.com.au

Images courtesy of clker.com.

www.stefkaharp.com

I am...

Contents

Acknowledgements v
Dedication vi
Introduction vii
I am alive 1
I am one with the Divine 2
I am a divine creation 4
I am a kind soul 6
I am the way 7
I am free from fear 8
I am free from anxiety 10
I am fearless 12
I am happy 13
I am in harmony 14
I am lovable 15
I do cherish my life 16
I am blessed and caressed 18
I do pray for peace 20
I express feelings 22
I am what I desire to be 24
I never stress 26
I am for peace 27

I have a life everlasting	28
I do forgive forever	30
I am the light	32
I trust myself	33
I am free from guilt	34
I am free from shame	36
I give the benefit of the doubt	38
I send out divine blessings	40
I do not perpetuate idleness	42
I know I am as God is	44
I aim not to blame	46
I respect myself	47
About the author	48

Acknowledgements

I wish to express my deep and sincere gratitude to my parents for teaching me the value of life — how to love and be happy as well as show kindness; and to my siblings, for being a part of my life.

My thanks, too, to the Australian Government for opening the door for me to migrate and become a permanent resident; to experience a different kind of life, culture and customs, which has been very enriching, enlightening and eye-opening. I am very grateful for the opportunity I have been given and guided to get to the point I am at.

Sincere gratitude to:

- my daughter for her patience and loving assistance in proofreading my work
- Alison Leader for her editing
- my publishing advisor for assistance given
- my niece Maria and my loyal friends who were willing to read my manuscripts and give constructive comments and feedback.

Dedication

Everything I write and have written so far is dedicated to my family and the divine within, which has guided me through life. At times my ignorance and oblivion to the facts revealed has led to strife and suffering. But these experiences have given me the much-needed fuel for my writings, and I hope they will help others. Life is like a jigsaw puzzle. Some things are meant to happen so that the pieces fit within that puzzle.

S.H.

I am ...

Introduction

Fear, Stefka believes, is a habit developed after a fearful experience, and perpetual dwelling on it and its associated feelings. The more thought given to the fear, the more energy released and the more powerful the fear becomes. Entrenched within, like a hungry monster needing to be fed with more fearful thoughts, fear is the biggest obstacle in life. As a result of fear we miss out on so many life opportunities, whether simply having fun, meeting people, a career, or a happy marriage. How much we miss out on depends on what kind of fear we have and how intense it is.

Stefka has had a variety of fears throughout her life. The accumulated anxiety of her fear was crushing her, but she would never admit it or show any outward signs. She thought it was a weakness to do so, but it felt as though a ghost had wrapped itself around her with a tight grip. She could hardly breathe.

Every time she tried something for the first time she faced the grip of fear. She would feel the tightness around her body. She felt paralysed, and could not move.

Once she started experimenting with making and breaking habits, she was on the way to freeing herself from the fears once and for all. To help herself in the process, Stefka wrote a couple of poems regarding fear and read them as often as the fear presented itself. Miracle of miracles happened! The fear became less intense with time, and one day it just wasn't there anymore. It had vanished. Once the energy regarding the fear was released, the fear was nullified. The feeling of not having to face the gripping fear was like breaking free from a confined space.

The poems included in this book deal with the topics of guilt, shame, blame and anxiety. You can, if you wish, develop affirmations of your own and say them when you feel a gripping fear come upon you.

For example:

- I nullify the fearful energy I created in the past and I am free.
- There is no more fear within me. I am free.
- I have no fear, and all is cool and calm.

Stefka Harp

Disclaimer: The author is expressing beliefs and views based on her life experience. There is no intention to offend anyone who has contrary views. The poems are fun to read and in the process can bring a positive and loving attitude.

I am ...

I love my life,

At long last and on time,
Make no question, I have come alive.

Affectionate to say the least,
Living life to the fullest,
I continue and ever so persist,
Vigorously, and I insist,
Everlasting love, serenity, peace.

Stefka Harp

I am a Divine creation, here to stay,

As is everyone out there, I dare to say,
Message I would like to convey.

Overjoyed I am to have a greeting,
None other, but with the Divine within,
Ever so present, an angel is fleeting.

Warmth fills my body at once,
I become elated fast,
Timeless soul for me to admire,
Holiness desired to transpire,

I am ...

The ultimate outcome upon me,
Hallelujah, it is time to be,
Embracing the true existence I can see.

Diligence is needed here,
Inevitable for me to hear,
Various thoughts created in my mind,
Illumination and passion I find,
Nothing but love and blessings I send out,
Everlasting peace and harmony is all about.

Stefka Harp

I am what I desire to be,

And besides, there are billions like me,
Mainly we need to realise and see

An angel leads the way to glee.

Dainty as divine creation would be,
Image and likeness of thee as it should,
Vivacious I am, as I possibly could.
Innermost strength with time,
Notably makes me feel alive,
Everlasting love makes me divine.

I am ...

Creation of innocence, shiny bright light,
Resembles the creator in its own right,
Eager to show the way,
At a loving pace every day.
Thoughts I nurture with delight,
Inkling of transformation overnight,
Overflow of love and peace to the world,
Neither to let go of the above,
        nor ever go to war.

Stefka Harp

I am a kind soul even if I say so,

Always and forever on the go,
Many moons have passed for sure,

At long last I am with the flow.

Knowledge and wisdom I have gained,
Invoking holiness to attain,
Never to turn back or resign,
Deep within peace I find.

Serving the holy of the holiest,
Oneness with the Divine is dearest,
Union, I declare it would last,
Love brings the best in me fast.

I am ...

I am open to the universe,

Affectionately for me to acquire,
More of divine energy to transpire.

Timeless universe is always there,
Harmonious and heavenly rare,
Elevation of the soul I would like to flair.

Willingly I choose to follow the light,
An angel scintillating in delight,
Yearning to become one with it ... it's my right.

Indeed I am quite clear,

An angel within is near,
Magical moment is here.

Fervent I am, as I have no fear,
Radiance shines from within so dear,
Effortlessly flows making me cheer,
Eternal silent voice I hear.

I am ...

Forgiveness is the core,
Reclaims peace forever more,
Overjoyed I am for the love bestowed,
Manifesting the Divine within, I adore.

Fair to say, if love is cherished,
Evidence that fear has perished,
At long last I am free,
Ray of hope upon me.

Stefka Harp

Immensely I delight, to

Acclaim my right,
Most of the time to look on the bright.

Fearful feelings to farewell, I
Reward myself even if I fail,
Enemy number one is my fear,
Endlessly creating anxiety to spear.

Forgiveness is a must to succeed,
Removes fear indeed.
Over and above I seek to
Master anxiety – for freedom to meet.

I am ...

Anyway, the above is not taken lightly, I
Nurture love and the free spirit nightly, I
Xero in without worry, my
Inner feelings tell a story,
Encouragement to go on.
The ultimate outcome for me is
Young forever and anxiety-free.

Stefka Harp

Invigorating feelings I dwell on,

Absolutely, for the fear to be gone,
Mighty cool and calm to be born.

Fear had been my obstacle for far too long,
Endeavouring I am not to let it prolong.
Awareness of it makes me get to the core,
Remembering that it is my mind for sure,
Largely creating the fear to flow.
Empowering myself not to react, I
Soothe the mind instead and concentrate,
Swiftly love and harmony to incorporate.

I am ...

Inside of me there is a happy child,

As adorable as I can be without denial,
Moment to cherish with a smile.

Heavens above send me happiness galore,
Always guiding me to more,
Pure energy of love to spare,
Plenty to go around, I declare,
Yes, for more happiness I prepare.

Innocence comes to the fore

Aiming to restore the
Manifesting life I adore.

Its magic I caress
Nifty way to be blessed.

Harmonious days ahead of me,
At long last where I would like to be.
Ready to unite with the Divine,
Miraculous transformation I find,
Onset for me to become alive,
Non-stop for me to shine.
Youth restored, leaving old age behind.

I am ...

I am sweet and serene,

Always, if I am to succeed,
My ultimate aim is to proceed.

Love and loving thoughts to the core, the
Only way peace and harmony to bestow,
Vivacious I am, uniting with the Divine,
Always gracefully to guide.
Brilliant white light upon me,
Lovable I am, you could see,
Embracing the divinity, hoping to be.

Stefka Harp

I am gentle with myself.

Diligently I walk the walk of life,
Onward only, to be precise.

Continually, without a rest,
Hearty wishes and all the best.
Enchanted my life is, I confess
Rejuvenation due to manifest
In its entirety, come what may.
Steadily coming and here to stay
Honesty I aspire to every day.

I am ...

My life ahead is a mystery,
Yesterday is a history.

Love and loving thoughts today,
Inevitable for me to pursue and pray.
Feelings of gladness for being alive
Enable me eternally to thrive.

It is a blessing to have a life,

A life of an eternal child
Merrily treading along with a smile.

Beaming with joy day and night,
Love to the world in its own right,
Everlasting peace in delight,
Sheer pleasure to know the light.
Satisfaction for the soul all the way,
Endless happiness every day,
Dazzling moments I am pleased to say.

An angel swiftly comes down,
Nobly looking around,
Delicate and humble all the way to the crown.

I am ...

Calmly I sit and wait
All the more to be caressed,
Receiving blessings which overflow,
Ever so peace to know.
Serenity upon me to restore,
Steady radiance to bestow,
Eternal holiness to know,
Delightful outcome for sure.

Stefka Harp

It is like this, prayer I say

Daily, anywhere,
Over and again with care.

Peace loving nature to bestow
Releasing peaceful thoughts galore
Aiming peace within to flow
Youthful body forever more.

I am ...

Forgiveness and prayer I come to know, is the
Only way to reach my goal, my
Reward is eternal happiness for sure.

Priority is to do it with all my heart,
Elevating the soul to feel such delight.
As I would like to see the light
Crowned around my head in a glow,
Evidence of inner peace and spiritual growth.

Stefka Harp

I sincerely declare

Emotions are very powerful dealings.
Xero in and acknowledge the feelings.
Priceless experience I do not dismiss,
Restoring the serenity to say the least.
Expressing my feelings sets me free,
Somewhere in my heart I agree
Strengthening the inner spirit to a degree.

I am ...

Forward only, past events I leave behind,
Enabling me to focus on here and now.
Establish what is holding me back and why.
Limitation to overcome with desire, for
Illuminating thoughts to aspire.
New skills to acquire with a prayer,
Gentleness to transpire and prepare
Spiritually to grow with loving care.

Stefka Harp

In the midst of being alive

Amazingly beautiful and wise, is the
Mighty glorious Divine.

With the best will in the world,
Heart and soul made of gold,
Attention to my thoughts I pay,
Transformation within I crave

In the here and now without delay.

I am ...

Dedication to my prayers for sure
Evidently comes to the fore.
Sheer pleasure to feel great and know
Inner-most self to explore,
Rejoicing in good health and
Embracing thoughts of wealth.

Today and every day I am bestowed with
Opportunity for spiritual growth, to

Be the person of my dreams and more,
Everlasting peace and harmony to the core.

Stefka Harp

I have found a way to de-stress.

Never to show off but to impress,
Everlasting love to thrill,
Vitality I would like to feel.
Emerging into a divine child,
Reclaiming my birth right with a smile.

Stressful situation, when I detect,
The truth of matter is I accept,
Ready to deal with it instead of react,
Eager to face the problem with respect.
Swift resolution comes and problem solved
Simple as that, and everything is resolved.

I am...

In its entirety I vow

Another day for me to know how
Motivation to acquire.

Forever more to inspire,
Overall peace to transpire,
Radiance upon that I desire.

Purity in my heart is
Essential for me to do it right.
Alliance with the Divine
Conquers, leaving worries behind,
Eternal peace I find.

Stefka Harp

I am blessed to have come to be,

Harmonious life upon me
Ascending as high as I could,
Voicing my feelings in hope
Ever so, to be of some good.

As I shall always uphold,

Life is a fine balanced act.
If enjoyed it would project
Fervent feelings as a matter of fact,
Essential for me to make a pact

I am ...

Eternally to give love and nothing else,
Virtue not to be ignored but caressed,
Esteem to reign in its glory
Rocketing sky-high reaching for the holy,
Laughing all the way.
Aiming for the divinity every day,
Sublime soul and more
Timeless faith to restore.
Innocence to come to the fore,
Necessary wisdom to flow
Gracefully bringing the desired glow.

Inevitable it is to forgive every day.

Dedication to the above I say,
Obediently, I do it, come what may.

Forgive, bless and I pray, the
Only way to feel gay
Rejoicing I am forever more, for
God grants me serenity for sure.
I am a soul divine, having a
Vibrant body in which it resides
Eternally, this makes me feel alive.

I am ...

Fortunate I am to have an inner guide,
Oneness to know and peace to find,
Radiance is the reward for being divine,
Enabling me to step back and
View my actions with respect.
Even so, to forgive is an ongoing task
Reunion with the timeless universe at last.

I vow to follow the light,

And become holy in my heart,
Magical moment could happen overnight.

Temptation I cannot resist,
Here on I have to persist,
Eternally until I exist.

Lost I might get on the way,
Instantly I begin to pray,
Gracious strength within to find,
Harmony and peace with time,
Tranquil self and divine glory is mine.

I am ...

I am trustworthy without doubt.

The time to trust myself is now.
Readily and sincerely I vow
Unconditionally without chatter,
Selecting thoughts that would matter
To bestow trust and clear the clatter.

Moreover I enjoy doing so,
Yearning to go on for sure,
Soothing the mind with calming words,
Empowering myself with loving thoughts,
Living my life focused on trust, without
Fail – eliminates the fear fast.

I am who I am no doubt.

Aspect I take into account,
Might as well, I talk about

Faithfully galloping along in amazement,
Rather hoping to be pleasant,
Expecting only the best,
Endless happiness to caress.

I am ...

Fresh start every morn'
Ready to embrace the dawn,
Opportunity to right the wrong,
Moment not to prolong

Grasp the wisdom of forgiveness I must,
Undoubtedly do it at once, for
Infinite love to freely flow,
Love everlasting and guilt no more,
Tranquillity in life for sure.

Infinite blessings out I pour,

Aiming to reach the world.
Make no mistake, take my word.

First and foremost forgiveness I ask for,
Redemption granted, I am sure.
Energy surging makes me feel free,
Enemy to be blessed on count of three ...

Furthermore, prayer is due,
Requesting happiness to be in view,
Onwards to nullify wrongdoing,
Moment of truth to cherish ongoing.

I am ...

So there is no shame in living my life.
Heavens above made me alive.
Away with the shame with all my heart,
Matter of fact it feels right, I
Envisage nothing but utter delight.

Stefka Harp

I am eternally divine.

Gracious soul and kind,
Impose self-discipline with time.
Various thoughts on my mind
Endless well-wishes for everyone to find.

Today is the time to make changes,
Here on I make sure
Ever trust to bestow.

Believe in self and others I must,
Endearing love I feel at once,
Necessary for the soul to bloom, I
Envisage happiness instead of gloom.
Furthermore I release happy thoughts
Infinitely, I do not stop.
Try it, miraculously it might just work.

I am ...

Only true love never doubts,
Fair to say without losing ground.

Today is the day, I
Hold dear and pray
Eagerly, without delay.

Dawn comes, I am up and on the way,
Only one thing to convey.
Unconditional love I send out,
Blessings, gratitude and trust all about,
To give the benefit of the doubt.

Stefka Harp

It is important for me to persist.

Spiritually to exist,
Endless loving thoughts sent out,
Never to turn back or doubt,
Dedication to the Divine is all about.

Out my loving thoughts go,
Unfailing they flow,
Tender feelings to bestow.

Delighted I am in sending blessings
Instantly, and forever progressing,
Vowing to release them out there,
Invigorating the world and self by releasing
Non-stop loving thoughts.
Effort rewarded with spiritual growth.

I am ...

Beyond all questions, thoughts are energies.
Loving thoughts would graciously
Empower the soul to let go of the scare,
Soothing the mind with a rapid flair.
Steady shift of thinking required,
Important awareness should be acquired,
Necessary for the soul to thrive,
Gratitude for being alive,
Satisfaction for the Divine.

I am always on the go,

Divine mission for me to explore,
Occasion for faith in me to restore.

Now and forever I would happily thrive,
Onset of abundance in life,
Time for me to find the Divine.

Paramount is to keep zooming
Even when I don't feel like moving.
Reasonable advice to explore,
Persist I do, and make changes as I go.
Eager to get to the core, loving
Thoughts released galore,
Unconditional love sent out with delight.
Approaching new ventures with all my heart,
The idleness fades away overnight,
Everlasting harmony by daylight.

I am ...

In no time, I am on my way,
Determination within every day.
Loving thoughts are the clue,
Ensuring love divine to pursue.
Necessary for me to proceed
Endlessly without stress indeed, it's a
Sheer joy for being blessed, with
Supreme creativity to express.

Stefka Harp

Innocent forever more,

Kind all the way to the core,
Noble and gracious for sure.
Only way to thrive,
Warmth within is making me alive.

Inside of me a feeling of celebration.

Always bringing illumination
Manifesting enjoyment and soul elevation.

I am ...

As the nature intended for me,
So to speak, that's how I turn to be.

Good and caring from inception
Overall is my perception,
Dreaming of one's perfection.

Instead I am happy
Seemingly the way I am.

Stefka Harp

I have a forgiving nature within.

Aiming destiny to fulfil,
Indeed, who said what I forgive
Merit upon me for not being naive.

Nightly I pray for those involved,
Onward only, I do not get embroiled.
Tranquillity embraces me as a reward.

Transition for the best on the way,
Occasion to keep evil at bay.

Being responsible for my actions,
Loving thoughts change the projection,
Attracting what I desire, else if I blame,
Massive energy lost, what a shame,
Embezzled emotions of the same attained.

I am ...

I am attuned to the Divine

    Regardless of who says what.
    Embracing myself for who I am,
    Something not to be neglected,
    Passion for it I have detected,
    Expecting a divine connection,
    Caressing the idea of respect to find
    Tender loving thoughts on my mind.

    May love, trust and respect
    Yield my way, to connect
    Sincere union with the universe.
    Endless joy and to be wise.
    Likewise in time, if I
    Follow my heart, respect I should find.

Stefka Harp

About the author

Stefka was born during World War II in a small village tucked away in the foothills of a big mountain in Eastern Macedonia.

Her family, like others in the village, gained their food from the land. It was a self-sufficient household. This lifestyle built much confidence in her and her siblings.

She migrated to Australia in 1972, where she still resides. She finished her degree, and a diploma in counselling, and gained jobs in the welfare sector.

The last seven years before retirement were spent in the DV sector. While working with people she noticed the power of thought in relation to destiny. She believes that when people change their thinking and implement positive and loving thoughts, life changes for better. Prayer, forgiveness, hope and faith go hand in hand with a positive attitude.

Academic achievements

Diploma of Community Services Management
    Southbank Institute of TAFE 2006

Diploma in Counselling
    Australian Institute of Counsellors 1993–1994

Bachelor of Arts Degree (Major Psychology)
    University of Queensland 1989

Economics, book keeping & accounting
    Business Studies College (Macedonia)

www.ingramcontent.com/pod-product-compliance
Lightning Source LLC
Chambersburg PA
CBHW061257040426
42444CB00010B/2402